LEVERS

ANGELA ROYSTON

Heinemann Library
Chicago, Illinois

© 2001 Heinemann Library
a division of Reed Elsevier Inc.
Chicago, Illinois

Customer Service 888-454-2279
Visit our website at www.heinemannlibrary.com

Designed by Visual Image
Illustrations by Barry Atkinson
Originated by Dot Gradations
Printed in China

05 04 03
10 9 8 7 6 5 4 3 2 1

Library of Congress Cataloging-in-Publication Data
Royston, Angela.
        Levers / Angela Royston.
                p. cm. – (Machines in action)
        Includes bibliographical references and index.
        Summary: Explains how levers work, describes different machines that uses levers, and tells how to create an example of a lever in a pop-up card.
        ISBN 1-57572-319-0 (HC), 1-4034-4084-0 (Pbk.)
        1. Levers—Juvenile literature. 2. Simple machines—Juvenile literature. [1. Levers.] I. Title. II. Series.

TJ147 .R86 2000
621.8'11—dc21

                                                                    00-035002

Acknowledgments
The author and publishers are grateful to the following for permission to reproduce copyright material: Cumulus / Trevor Clifford, pp. 8, 15, 18, 22, 23; Garden and Wildlife Matters, p. 10; Heinemann / Trevor Clifford, pp. 4, 7, 11, 14, 17, 20, 21, 23, 24, 28, 29; Impact / Piers Cavendish, p. 5; Pictor Uniphoto, p. 25; Robert Harding Picture Library, p. 16; Telegraph Colour Library / Space Frontiers Ltd., p. 27; Tony Stone Images / Don Spiro, p. 12, Tony Stone Images / Joe Cornish, p. 19; Travel Ink / Tony Page, p. 9.

Cover photograph reproduced with permission of Milepost 92½.

Some words are shown in bold, **like this.** You can find out what they mean by looking in the glossary.

CONTENTS

What Do Levers Do?

Using a hammer as a lever, only a small amount of effort is needed to pull a nail out.

How can you make yourself stronger than you are? The answer is by using a machine. Some machines are complicated and use a motor or engine to give them power. A few machines are so simple you might not think of them as "machines." Levers, wheels, screws, springs, ramps, and pulleys are simple machines that have been used for thousands of years.

This book is about levers. A lever is a long, thin rod or stick that can be used to move things. It is often used to lift weights, to balance weights, and to cut things.

Think about it!

Look at the picture of the road work below. The wheelbarrow and the shovel are two levers that you can learn about in this book.

Builders use many kinds of levers to help them lift things and move things.

Lifting the world

A lever is extraordinarily powerful. With a simple lever you could lift an enormous elephant. Archimedes was a Greek who lived nearly 2,300 years ago. He worked out the scientific law that governs how levers work and said, "Give me a place to stand, and I will move the Earth."

5

How a Lever Works

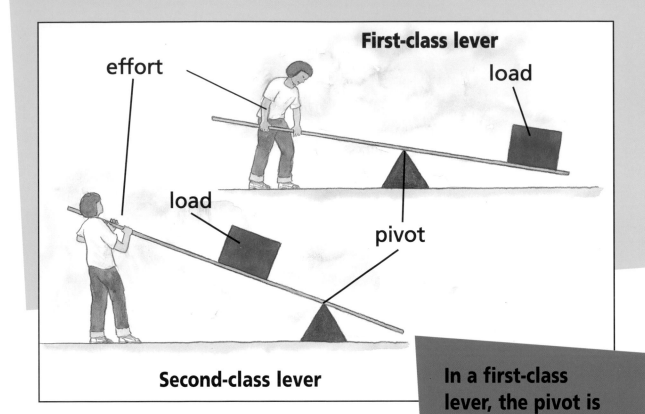

effort

First-class lever

load

load

pivot

Second-class lever

To move something, you have to push it or pull it. The **force** used in the push or pull is called the **effort**. The thing you want to move is called the **load**.

The pivot

A lever works by turning around a point, called the **pivot**. In the pictures above, the pivot is the block of wood that supports the lever. As the effort moves one end of the lever down, the end on the other side of the pivot moves up. The load is easiest to lift when the effort is as far as possible from the pivot and the load is close to the pivot.

In a first-class lever, the pivot is between the effort and the load. In a second-class lever, the load is between the pivot and the effort.

Try this!

You will need one thick book (the load), a wooden block (the pivot), and three strong rulers—a short one, a medium length one, and a very long one. One at a time, put each ruler over the pivot and place the book on one end. Push the other end of the ruler down. Which ruler needs the least effort to lift the book? Which lever needs the most effort?

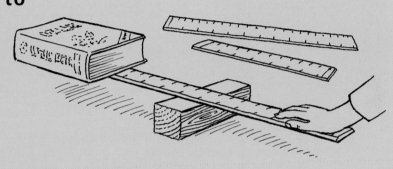

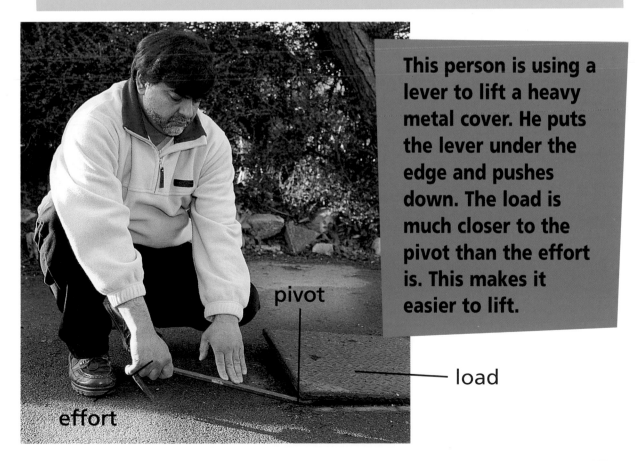

pivot

effort

load

This person is using a lever to lift a heavy metal cover. He puts the lever under the edge and pushes down. The load is much closer to the pivot than the effort is. This makes it easier to lift.

Stronger Than You Think

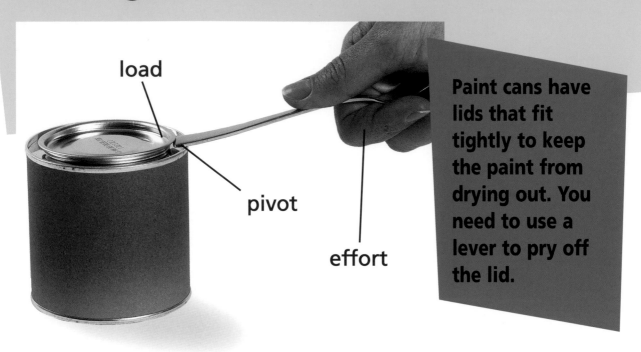

load

pivot

effort

Paint cans have lids that fit tightly to keep the paint from drying out. You need to use a lever to pry off the lid.

A lever changes a small **force** into a big one. It would be very difficult to get a lid off a paint can using just your fingers. But, if you put the end of a spoon underneath the lid and push down gently you can lift the lid.

Less effort

A long spoon makes lifting even easier because it spreads out the **effort** of lifting. Your hand moves a long distance to lift the **load** (the lid) a short way. The farther away the effort is from the **pivot**, the less effort is needed.

A wheelbarrow makes lifting easier because you lift the handles farther than you lift the load. The wheelbarrow in the photo is a **second-class lever**. The load is between the pivot and the effort.

8

Think about it!

The longer a lever, the easier it is to lift the load, so why doesn't a wheelbarrow have handles that are six feet long? What would happen then? Why does a wheelbarrow have only one wheel? What would be the advantages and disadvantages of having three or four wheels?

A wheelbarrow is a lever. When it is full, the gardener lifts the handles to move the load. The wheelbarrow's pivot is the center of the wheel. The wheel helps the wheelbarrow move forward easily.

load

effort

pivot

Changing Pull to Push

Digging earth is hard work, but using a pitchfork as a lever makes it easier. What kind of lever is the pitchfork?

It is easier to push down than to pull up. A lever changes pull to push. A pitchfork, for example, makes it possible to lift up by pushing down. You push the pitchfork into the earth and then push the handle down (the **effort**) to lift up the earth (the **load**). It is not always easy to see where the **pivot** is. In this example, the pivot is where the pitchfork rests against the ground. What other garden tools are used as levers?

Make it work!

Imagine you have a lot of bags that you need to take upstairs. Draw a design for a lever to help you lift your bags up the stairs instead of carrying them. Your lever will need a pivot, a handle, and a special end to carry your bags.

The tip of the bottle opener pivots on the cap to lift the rim.

push down

pull up

Bottle opener

The bottle opener is a **second-class lever**. The pivot is the tip of the opener which rests on the cap. The claw catches on the cap (the load) and pulls it up.

Oars and Paddles

Levers can help you move more easily and quickly through the water. A rowboat has two levers (the oars) which pivot at the **oarlocks**. Is the oar a **first-class lever** or a **second-class lever**?

In a row boat, the rower leans back to pull the boat forward through the water. The oarlock keeps the oar from slipping along the edge of the boat. What else does it do?

Sometimes everything in boats seems backwards. The rower faces backward in order to go forward. With an oar, the **effort** is closer to the **pivot** than the **load** (the water). It would take less effort if it were the other way around, but what would happen then? In rowing, you pull a short way to move the boat a long way through the water.

load

effort

pivot

Canoes

A paddle is a lever too. But it is neither a first-class nor a second-class lever. As the canoeist pulls the paddle through the water it pivots around the upper hand. In this case, the effort (the lower hand) is between the pivot and the load (the part of the paddle in the water). A paddle is an example of a **third-class lever**.

The paddle is a third-class lever. The effort (the hand) moves a short way to make the load move a long way.

Think about it!

Suppose you found a boat but it had no oars or paddles. The only things you could use as a paddle were a broom, a frying pan, a shovel, and a tennis racket. Which would make the best paddle? What other things would make good paddles?

Balancing Act

Levers can be used to make things balance. In a balance scale, the rod that joins the two **pans** is a lever. It **pivots** in the center; each pan is the same distance from the pivot. The pans balance when the **effort** (the weights) equals the **load** (the object being weighed).

To find out how much something weighs, add weights to one pan until they balance the object in the other pan.

The woman is heavier than the child. What can they do to balance the seesaw?

The seesaw

The seesaw is also a lever that pivots in the center. If two children who are about the same weight sit at each end, the seesaw will be balanced. If one child sits closer to the pivot, his effort (weight) will have less effect and the seesaw will go up at that end. If one child is heavier than the other, the seesaw will go down at her end.

Seesaws in parks and playgrounds usually use springs to help to keep the seesaw balanced. This means the children do not have to be exactly the same weight to balance the seesaw.

Try this!

Make a seesaw using a ruler and a triangular block for the pivot. Put other small blocks on each side of the seesaw. How many ways can you get two blocks to balance one block?

Tower Crane

The crane driver lowers the hook at the end of the long cable to pick up a heavy load.

The tower crane uses the laws of levers to balance its **load**. The **boom** of the tower crane **pivots** around the driver's cab. Can you see the big block on the short end of the boom, behind the driver? The block is called a **counterweight** because it balances the weight of the load.

The counterweight is nearer to the pivot than the load so it has to be much heavier than the load. When the crane picks up a very heavy load, the driver moves the hook closer to the cab to balance the load.

Think about it!

Suppose that the crane driver puts down a heavy load of metal beams and then picks up a lighter load of window frames. Which way should he move the hook—towards the cab or away from it?

A mobile

Look at the top rod of the mobile. Four shapes are hanging from one end, and only two are hanging from the other end. The top rod is balanced because the pivot (the thread it is hanging from) is closer to the heavier end.

Each rod of the mobile hangs by a thread tied to the rod above. Each rod acts as a lever that pivots around the knot of the thread.

Bridges

When a boat or ship is taller than a bridge, the bridge must be lifted to let the boat through. The bridge across the canal is attached to a lever. When the handle of the lever is pulled down, the other end lifts up one side of the bridge. The person pulling the lever is helped by a heavy weight on the end of the lever handle. The weight balances the weight of the bridge. The person only has to add a small amount of **effort** to lift the bridge.

Using a lever and a counterweight, one person can lift the bridge.

Tower Bridge in London is in two halves. When a tall ship needs to pass through it, the traffic is cleared and each half swings up.

Tower Bridge

Each side of Tower Bridge weighs about 1,000 tons! Heavy weights on the outer end of each side balance the weight. **Electric motors** are used to lift the bridge. The **counterweights** are so accurate that the motors used to lift the bridge are very small–they are the same size as the motors used in lawn mowers.

Try this!

Make a model to show how Tower Bridge works. Use short rulers for the two parts of the bridge. Place each on a support, such as a wooden block, and position them so that they just touch. Use modeling clay to balance the weight of the rulers. Can you make your bridge strong enough to hold a small model car?

Scissors and Wire Cutters

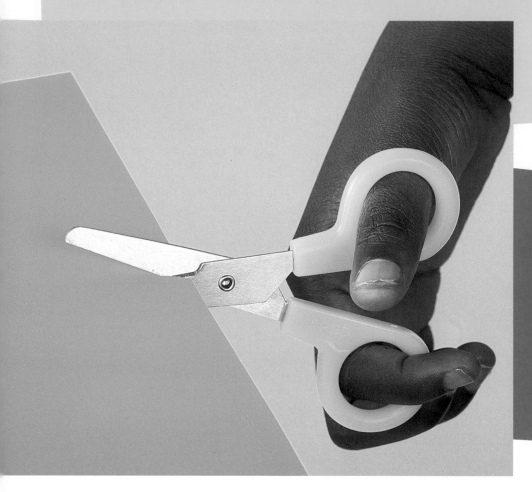

Scissors are a double lever. Squeezing the handles together gives a strong force between the blades.

A pair of scissors is useful for cutting paper, cloth, and other things. Scissors may not look like levers, but they are. In fact, they are not just one lever, but two levers working together. The **pivot** is in the middle, so each lever is a **first-class lever**.

As you squeeze the handles together (the **effort**), the blades are pushed together to cut the paper. The scissors have short handles and long blades. This makes it easier to control the amount the scissors cut. Always be careful not to cut yourself when you use scissors.

20

Try this!

Test a pair of scissors to see which part of the blade cuts the best. Cut a piece of thin cardboard with the tip of the blades, the middle of the blades, and lastly with the part of the blades nearest to the pivot. Which part cuts best? Try several pairs of scissors to see if you get the same result each time. Can you explain what you find out? Be careful when testing sharp-pointed scissors.

This engineer is using a pair of wire cutters. The cutters are so powerful they can cut through thick wire and even metal rods.

Wire cutters

The wire cutters have long handles and short blades. The effort which the **engineer** applies to the handles is much farther from the pivot than the wire he is cutting (the **load**). He only has to use a small effort to get a strong **force** between the blades.

Pliers and Nutcrackers

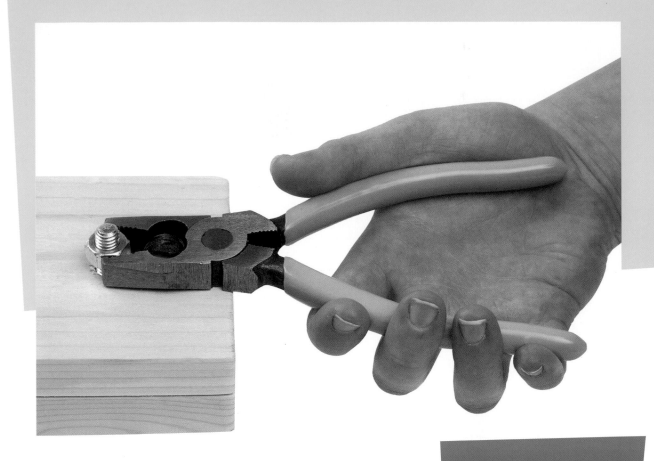

Pliers are double levers that are used to grip things tightly. Squeezing the handles produces a strong **force** between the jaws. The jaws have many grooves that help the pliers grip without slipping.

The pliers are designed so that the jaws always grip the nut squarely. This is different from a pair of scissors, where the blades meet in the shape of a "V."

Pliers are useful for unscrewing a tight nut. The handles provide a long lever and the pliers grip the nut tightly.

Think about it!

Tweezers are double levers too. What kind of double levers are they?

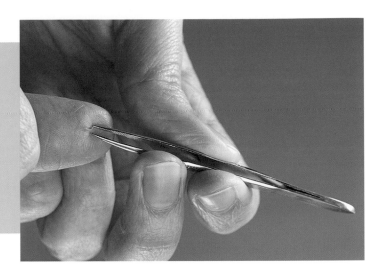

Nutcrackers

Nutcrackers are second-class double levers. The **load** is between the handles, and the **pivot** is at the end. Nutcrackers are shaped to hold either a small nut or a large nut, such as a walnut. When you squeeze the handles, the nutcracker magnifies your **effort**. The handles are levers that pivot at the end and squeeze the walnut until it cracks.

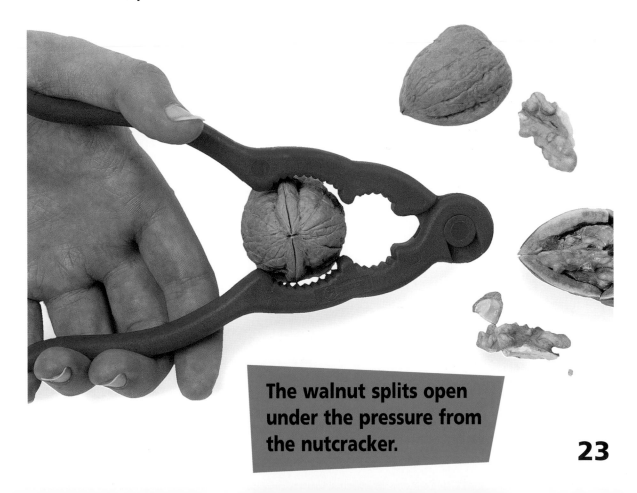

The walnut splits open under the pressure from the nutcracker.

23

Levers That Push Levers

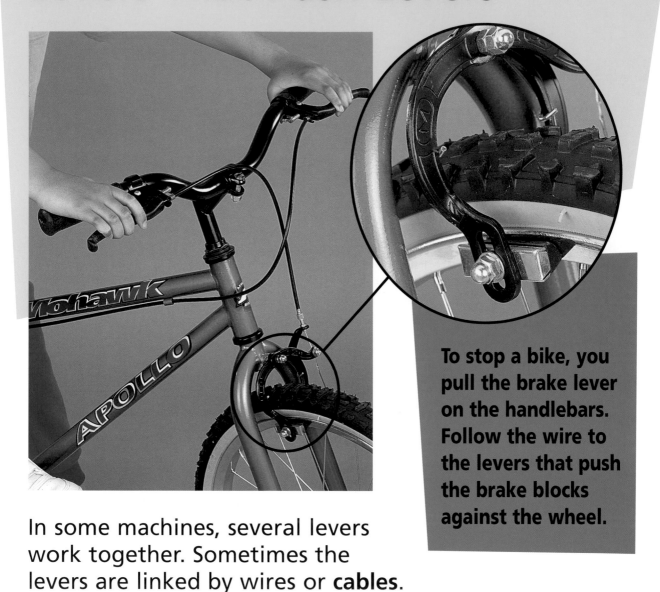

To stop a bike, you pull the brake lever on the handlebars. Follow the wire to the levers that push the brake blocks against the wheel.

In some machines, several levers work together. Sometimes the levers are linked by wires or **cables**.

There are two brake levers on the handlebars of a bicycle. One works the brakes on the back wheel, and the other works the brakes on the front wheel. Each brake lever is joined to metal **calipers** by a strong wire. When you pull the brake lever, the wire pulls the metal calipers on each side of the wheel. The calipers push the **brake blocks** against the rim of the wheel, which makes the wheel slow down.

Did you know?

An excavator uses hydraulic power to move its levers. Hydraulic power works by forcing oil through a narrow tube. It is another way of turning a small force into a large one. To see how this works, squeeze the end of a hose while water is running through it. The water shoots out more powerfully when the end is small.

boom

dipper

In an excavator, three main levers work together to guide the bucket.

Excavators

The excavator arm has three parts—the **boom**, the dipper, and the bucket. The boom raises and lowers the dipper. The dipper **pivots** where it joins the boom. It moves the bucket backward and forward. The bucket tilts up and down to dig and to empty.

Piano Keys

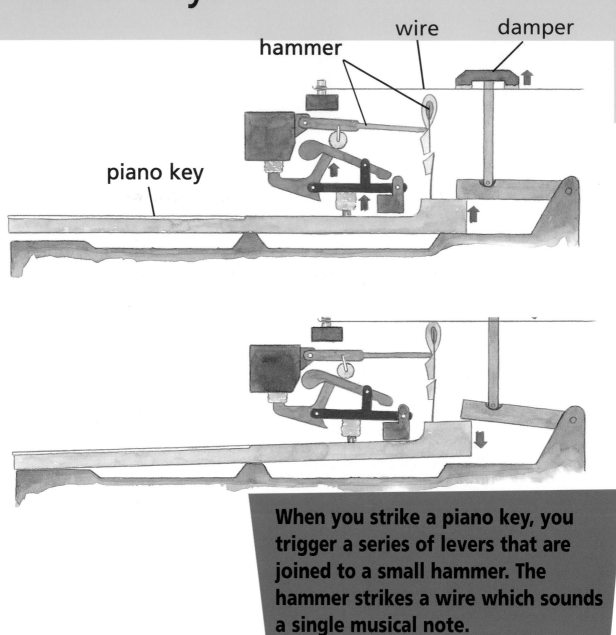

wire

damper

hammer

piano key

When you strike a piano key, you trigger a series of levers that are joined to a small hammer. The hammer strikes a wire which sounds a single musical note.

Each key on a grand piano is joined to a hammer that strikes a particular note. The sound is made by the **vibrations** of a tight wire. When you release the key, a **damper** moves down to stop the wire from vibrating. If it didn't, the note would go on sounding, as it does when you hold the key down.

Striking a note

A small movement on the piano key lifts the red lever. This lifts the orange lever and the hammer. The hammer strikes the wire above. The levers change the small movement of the key to a large movement of the hammer. At the same time the green lever at the end of the key lifts the damper off the wire to let it vibrate.

When you take your finger off the piano key, the hammer moves smoothly down. The damper drops back onto the wire to stop the sound. A pianist can play notes quickly and clearly because the system works so smoothly.

Think about it!

The space shuttle's robot arm is a series of levers. It is used to move satellites in or out of the spacecraft's loading bay. Only a small effort is needed to work the arm in space. Why do you think that is so?

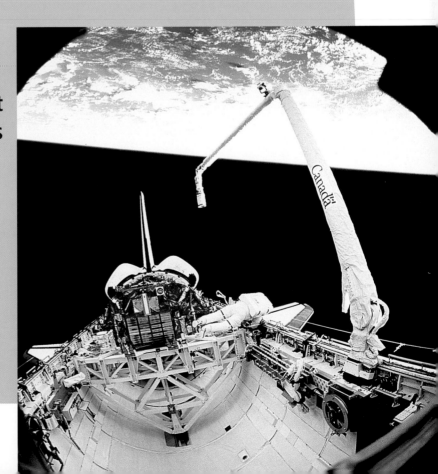

Make a Pop-up Card

A hidden lever pushes the clown's legs and arms up and down.

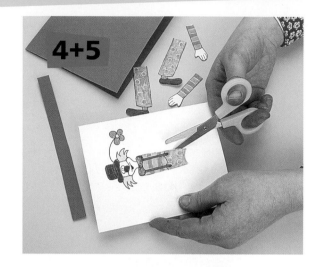

You will need:

- a large piece of thick paper or posterboard
- 2 paper fasteners
- colored pens, a pencil, scissors, glue

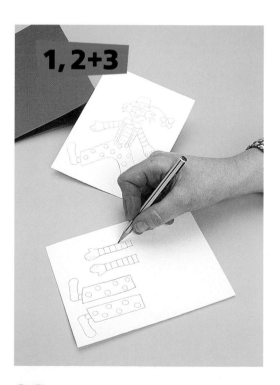

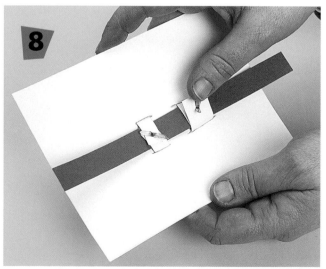

1   Cut a piece of thick paper 12 inches by 8 inches. Fold it down the middle to create a card that is 6 inches wide and 8 inches long.

2   Cut another piece of paper 5 inches wide by 7 inches long. On it draw the head and body of a clown.

3   On a spare piece of paper, draw the legs and arms. Make them longer than you want them to appear on the finished card.

4   Cut a slider 3/4 inch wide and 8 inches long.

5   Color in all the parts of the clown. Cut vertical slots in the body of the clown where the arms and legs should go.

6   Push the arms and legs through the slots and turn them to point down. Turn the clown over.

7   Place the slider over the back of the clown so 1/2 inch shows above and below the paper. Mark where the arms and legs meet the slider. Trim them if they are too long.

8   Make a hole through the slider and through each of the arms and push a paper fastener through. Make another hole through the slider and the top of each of the legs and push the other paper fastener through.

9   Put glue around the edge of the paper, but not where the slider crosses it.

10 Carefully glue the clown inside the card.

11 When the glue is dry, pull the slider to see the clown's arms and legs lift up.

Glossary

boom long arm of a crane or excavator to which a hook or bucket is attached

brake block rubber block that rubs against a bicycle wheel to slow it down

cable thick wire

caliper metal arm

counterweight weight that balances a load

damper lever that stops the sound of a note made by a piano key

effort using energy to do something

electric motor engine that uses electricity to move something

engineer someone who designs or works with machines, bridges, and other technical things

excavator machine used for moving earth

force push or pull that makes something move

first-class lever lever in which the pivot is between the effort and the load

hydraulic power force produced by liquid being squeezed in a thin tube

leverage ability to act as a lever

load weight that a lever moves or balances

oarlock metal peg which supports and holds the oar in a row boat

pans balance scales have two pans, one to hold the weights and the other to hold the load

pivot point on a lever around which the lever turns, or the act of a lever turning around that point

second-class lever lever in which the load is between the pivot and the effort

third-class lever lever in which the effort is between the load and the pivot

vibrations small, fast movements backwards and forwards

Answers to Questions

p. 7   The longest ruler should lift the books most easily. The shortest ruler should need the most effort.

p. 9   Very long handles would make it awkward to push the wheelbarrow around corners and difficult to tip it up to empty it. Three or four wheels would mean that you would not have to lift the wheelbarrow to push it, but the wheels would be more likely to get stuck in wet mud and loose ground.

p. 10   A pitchfork is a first-class lever. A spade, trowel, and hoe are levers too.

p. 12   An oar is a first-class lever.

p. 12   Photo: The oarlock supports the oar and acts as the pivot.

p. 12   If the oarlock were closer to the water than to the rower's hand, each stroke would take very little effort. However, the end of the oar in the water would not move very far, and neither would the boat.

p. 13   A shovel has a long handle and a wide end. It would make the best paddle because it would push the most water on each stroke.

p. 15   The woman should move closer to the pivot in the middle of the seesaw.

p. 17   When the driver picks up a lighter load he should move the hook away from the cab. He can also move the counterweight closer to the cab.

p. 21   The part of the blades nearest the pivot cut best because the effort is strongest there.

p. 23   Tweezers are third-class double levers. The effort is between the pivot and the load.

p. 27   Satellites are weightless in space so the space shuttle's robot arm works on very little power.

Index

More Books to Read

Dahl, Michael. *Levers.* Danbury, Conn.: Children's Press, 1996.

Grimshaw, Catherine. *Machines.* Chicago: World Book Inc., 1998.

Oxlade, Chris. *Science Magic with Machines.* Hauppage, N.Y.: Barron's Educational Series, Inc., 1995.